OUR FUTURE IN SPACE

SPACE TOURISTS
VACATIONS ACROSS THE UNIVERSE

David Jefferis

Crabtree Publishing Company
www.crabtreebooks.com

INTRODUCTION

Could you take a space vacation in future? There are plenty of enthusiasts aiming to make this exciting dream come true, but it's still early days for private spaceflight. So for the time being, a ticket to space will be a very special, high-priced item.

However, pioneer companies such as Blue Origin, SpaceX, and Virgin Galactic are working to perfect the technology that's needed. In the future, space tourists may have a choice of a space joyride, a trip to a space hotel, or maybe even a flight to the Moon or beyond. Read on for more!

↑ Companies such as SpaceX (above) and Blue Origin compete to create technology that will fly tourists into space.

🌳 Crabtree Publishing Company
www.crabtreebooks.com   1-800-387-7650

Written and produced for Crabtree Publishing by:
David Jefferis

Technical advisor:
Mat Irvine FBIS (Fellow of the British Interplanetary Society)

Editors:
Mat Irvine, Janine Deschenes

Prepress Technicians:
Mat Irvine, Ken Wright

Proofreader:
Petrice Custance

Print Coordinator:
Margaret Amy Salter

Acknowledgements
We wish to thank all those people who have helped to create this publication and provided images.
Individuals:
    Frank Hampson/Eagle
    David Jefferis
    Gavin Page
    Pat Rawlings/NASA
    Keith Tarrier/Fotolia
Organizations:
    Bake in Space GmBH
    Bigelow Aerospace
    Blue Origin
    Boeing Corp
    Canadian Space Agency
    ESA European Space Agency

Houston Spaceport
    JPL Jet Propulsion Laboratory
    Lockheed Martin Space
      Systems
    NASA Space Agency
    NASDA, JAXA, Japanese
      Space Agencies
    Obayashi Corp
    Roscosmos Russian Space
      Agency
    Sierra Nevada Corp
    SpaceX
    The Spaceship Company
    Thoth Technology
    Virgin Galactic
    XPrize Foundation

Printed in the USA/102017/CG20170907

Library and Archives Canada Cataloguing in Publication

Jefferis, David, author
     Space tourists / David Jefferis.

(Our future in space)
Includes index.
Issued in print and electronic formats.
ISBN 978-0-7787-3536-6 (hardcover).--
ISBN 978-0-7787-3548-9 (softcover).--
ISBN 978-1-4271-1942-1 (HTML)

    1. Space tourism--Juvenile literature. 2. Interplanetary voyages--Juvenile literature. 3. Outer space--Civilian use--Juvenile literature. I. Title.

TL794.7.J44 2017   j338.4'7910919   C2017-905188-1
                                        C2017-905189-X

Library of Congress Cataloging-in-Publication Data

Names: Jefferis, David, author.
Title: Space tourists / David Jefferis.
Description: New York, New York : Crabtree Publishing Company,
    [2018] | Series: Our future in space | Includes index.
Identifiers: LCCN 2017044200 (print) | LCCN 2017045348 (ebook) |
    ISBN 9781427119421 (Electronic HTML) |
    ISBN 9780778735366 (reinforced library binding : alk. paper) |
    ISBN 9780778735489 (pbk. : alk. paper)
Subjects: LCSH: Space tourism--Juvenile literature. | Manned space
    flight--Juvenile literature.
Classification: LCC TL793 (ebook) | LCC TL793 .J438 2018 (print) |
    DDC 910.919--dc23
LC record available at https://lccn.loc.gov/2017044200

CONTENTS

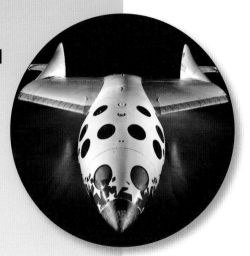

TICKET TO SPACE

Space tourism started in 2001, with a privately-funded visit to the International Space Station.

Soyuz spacecraft attached to one end of the ISS

→ What do the words "space tourist" really mean?

They describe a citizen who pays for space travel personally, rather than being sponsored by an official agency, such as a government. Seven space tourists flew to space from 2001 to 2009, each paying from $20 to $40 million to stay for a week on the **International Space Station** (ISS).

← The mission patch worn by Dennis Tito on his space suit.

→ Who was the first space tourist?

An American engineer, Dennis Tito. He showed that good health and fitness are more important than youth, as he was 60 years old when he stayed on the ISS.

← Dennis Tito (far left) flew to the ISS with the Soyuz Commander, Talgat Musabayev (middle), and Flight Engineer, Yury Baturin.

→ How long was Tito on board the ISS?

His time on the ISS lasted for 7 days, 22 hours, 4 minutes. During this time, the station circled Earth 128 times, completing each **orbit** in about 90 minutes. The ISS travels around Earth at a speed of about 17,000 mph (27,350 km/h).

→ How did he get to the ISS?

Tito flew to the ISS in the Russian Soyuz TM-32 spacecraft. He returned in the TM-31, which was already **docked** at the ISS, having previously taken a crew of three there.

Solar panels make electricity from sunlight

> → The Soyuz has three sections, or modules. In front is the orbital module, which docks to the ISS. Behind this is the descent module, in which the crew sits. The rear service module has solar panels, which supply electricity.

→ Is the Soyuz a new design?

No; it's a three-seat spacecraft that dates from 1966, though there have been many upgrades since then. The latest version, the Soyuz MS, first flew in 2016. It will be in regular service until at least the mid-2020s.

5

TRAINING FOR SPACE

Dennis Tito and other space tourists have trained hard with professional astronauts, before leaving for the ISS.

British astronaut Tim Peake sets off a rescue flare

➜ Why is training so important?

Space flight is difficult on the human body. It means undergoing acceleration during takeoff, which may be up to 5G or more. 5G describes five times the force of **gravity**, meaning five times your normal weight. In space, you float **weightless**, in free fall. Returning from orbit involves more stress and strain, until the "thump" of landing.

↑ In this test, the Belgian astronaut Frank de Winne jumps from a Soyuz crew module. A diver checks to make sure he stays safe.

➜ What happens after landing?

If all goes well, recovery teams collect a spacecraft crew quickly. But training also prepares for a spacecraft that goes off-course. A Soyuz **capsule** normally lands in central Asia, but a reentry error could mean coming down in the sea, or even in a jungle. So astronauts need training for all possible events.

A typical experience flight provides several weightless periods

Airline seats removed inside the main cabin

A300

noverspace cnes

European astronauts practice inside the A300

⬆ This Airbus A300 is used for repeated roller-coaster style flights. These flights give passengers about 30 seconds of weightlessness.

➔ **Will future tourists have to train as thoroughly as this?**
Companies such as Virgin Galactic and Blue Origin aim for exciting, but brief trips to the edge of space. Training for these is quicker and easier than for longer flights to the International Space Station.

This Boeing space suit is designed to be lightweight and comfortable

WOULD TOURISTS NEED TO BE SUPER-FIT?

For joyrides to the edge of space, you will need to be no more than reasonably fit and healthy, and be able to pass simple medical checks.

Even so, you'll need to prepare properly beforehand, just as you would for a skiing or diving trip. So a daily exercise routine for several weeks beforehand should be on the "must-do" list for any space tourist.

7

FLYING BEYOND OUR WORLD

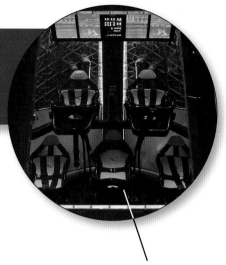

Space starts at an invisible boundary between air and space, known as the **Karman line.**

Inside the SpaceX Crew Dragon

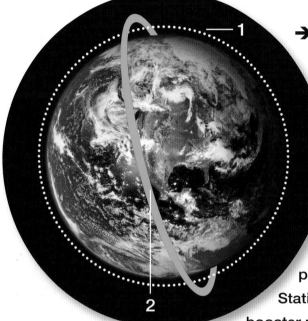

→ What is the Karman line?

It's also called "the edge of space" and lies 62 miles (100 km) above Earth. There, the atmosphere is too thin for an aircraft to fly, so it is accepted as the boundary between air and space. Reaching the Karman line means that you have earned a pair of astronaut's "wings." They are a special badge that proves you have flown into space.

← The Karman line (1) is far lower than the orbital path (2) of the fast-moving International Space Station. The high speed of the ISS means that powerful booster rockets are needed to send astronauts there.

→ Who flies to the Karman line?

Space tourism companies, such as Blue Origin and Virgin Galactic, have designed craft to fly passengers there and back.

A ticket to the Karman line is at least 100 times cheaper than a week on the ISS. Even so, at $250,000 per seat, Karman flights are very expensive.

→ Will I be able to take a spaceflight one day?

It should be possible, especially when flights become common. Ticket prices may then become more affordable.

↑ A Blue Origin test ends with the safe return of a New Shepard launch rocket.

WHAT SPACECRAFT COULD I FLY ABOARD?

These spacecraft could be used for taking tourists on flights to space.

The Blue Origin space capsule (1) is built for trips to the Karman line, as is the Virgin Space Ship (VSS) (2).

The Boeing CST-100 (3) and Lockheed Martin Orion (4) will go to the ISS (5) and beyond. Professional astronauts will fly in them, but tourists may pay for rides one day. The SpaceX Crew Dragon (6) is a step in the company's plans for private flights to Earth orbit, the Moon, and Mars. The Dream Chaser spaceplane (7) will come in two versions, crewed and uncrewed.

WINNING THE XPRIZE

 The **Ansari XPRIZE** offered a $10 million reward for the first privately-funded flight that reached the Karman line.

Mike Melvill, the first private astronaut

→ What was the craft that flew to the Karman line first?

It was called *SpaceShipOne* (SS1), and was piloted by Mike Melvill, who became the first private astronaut on June 21, 2004, when he reached a height of 407 feet (124 m) above the Karman line. He opened a bag of candies at the top of the flight, and saw that in the weightless conditions there, they floated free in the cabin.

↑ **SS1 was lifted off the ground by the White Knight twin-jet carrier plane.**

→ Who won the Ansari XPrize?

Another pilot, Brian Binnie, flew a later flight to win the Ansari XPrize. This flight was the winner because the SS1 carried extra weight to simulate two passengers, which was a condition for winning the prize.

→ **Pilot's eye-view from *White Knight's* cockpit, which had the same layout as SS1.**

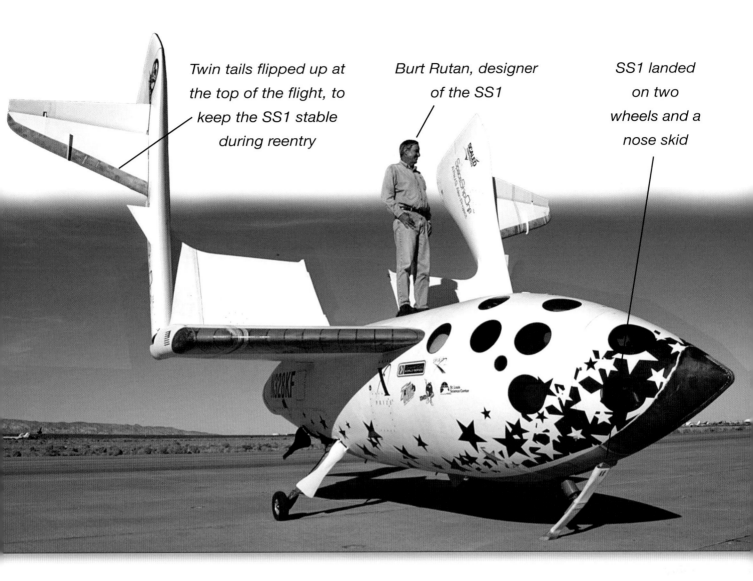

Twin tails flipped up at the top of the flight, to keep the SS1 stable during reentry

Burt Rutan, designer of the SS1

SS1 landed on two wheels and a nose skid

→ How was the SS1 powered?

It had a single rocket motor, which had enough fuel to operate for just under a minute-and-a-half. The *White Knight* carrier plane took SS1 to more than 8 miles (13 km) above the ground. The SS1 was then released to fly free. The pilot fired the rocket motor, and zoomed upward to hit a top speed of 2186 mph (3518 km/h).

↑ Burt Rutan was the man behind both the SS1 and its *White Knight* carrier plane.

WHERE IS SPACESHIPONE?

The SS1 is retired from flight duties, and on display to visitors at the National Air and Space Museum, Washington, DC.

On display near the SS1 is another famous flying machine, called The Spirit of St. Louis, which was flown by Charles Lindbergh across the Atlantic Ocean, in 1927.

→ Will another SS1 ever be built?

SS1's job was over when Brian Binnie won the XPrize. But the unique design was taken up by British businessman Richard Branson, founder of the Virgin Galactic space company. With this, Branson aims to create a premier space tourist carrier, by offering flights aboard the bigger, six-passenger *SpaceShipTwo*.

SPACESHIPTWO

Following the success of SpaceShipOne, its successor was designed to be more than twice the size.

Inspecting the crash site of the first SpaceShipTwo

→ What is SpaceShipTwo?

It's the spaceplane design that followed on from the successful SpaceShipOne. Five SS2s were ordered by Virgin Galactic, but the first one, called *Enterprise*, went out of control during a test flight in 2014. Sadly, the co-pilot, Michael Alsbury, was killed. A second SS2, called the Virgin Space Ship (VSS) *Unity* started tests in 2016.

⬇ **Maximum height for a VSS is 68 miles (110 km), just above the Karman line.**

→ Is VSS *Unity* safe to fly?

Like the SS1, it has a moving tail, often called a feather. Designer Burt Rutan included this feature to stabilize the plane during descent from space. He says it makes the craft at least as safe as airplanes of the 1920s.

→ How fast does a VSS fly?

A single rocket motor at the rear provides a massive push, to a top speed of 2500 mph (4000 km/h). A flight lasts more than two hours, though much of this time is taken up by the Virgin Mother Ship (VMS) carrier plane's slow climb to release the VSS, about 8.7 miles (14 km) above the ground.

Once released, the VSS climbs until its fuel is spent. Then it coasts upward to the Karman line, followed by a gliding flight down to a runway landing.

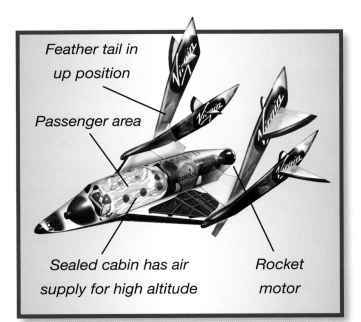

Feather tail in up position

Passenger area

Sealed cabin has air supply for high altitude

Rocket motor

→ **Up to six people plus two crew fly in a Virgin spaceplane. The big thrill is a few minutes of weightless floating at the top of the flight.**

WHAT COMES AFTER SPACESHIPTWO?

Virgin Galactic's founder, Richard Branson, has plenty of ideas for the future. The Spaceship Company builds the VSS spaceplanes and jet carriers to transport them to high altitude. There are plans for bigger orbital rockets, and also to develop a successor to the famed high-speed Concorde airliner. The new jet will be able to take 55 passengers from New York to London in three and a half hours.

BLUE ORIGIN BLASTS OFF

Jeff Bezos founded the internet company Amazon. He also masterminds Blue Origin, which rivals other space tourism pioneers with the New Shepard rocket system.

→ **How does the New Shepard rocket perform?**

Like SpaceShipTwo, New Shepard has a single rocket motor, but makes a vertical takeoff. New Shepard flew a test flight above the Karman line in 2015, carrying a circular space capsule similar to the later space tourist version.

For passenger flights, the capsule's "largest windows in space" give everyone on board an unbeatable view.

↑ Engine testing (1) for the Blue Origin New Shepard rocket, built to carry a six-seat tourist capsule (2). The capsule is fitted with very large windows (3, 4).

→ How long does a New Shepard flight take?

New Shepard accelerates from launch for about two and a half minutes. Then the capsule separates, and coasts silently up to the edge of space, where tourists can float freely in the cabin for a few minutes. Then the capsule begins its long fall back to Earth.

→ How does the New Shepard make a landing?

After separating from the capsule, New Shepard makes a powered landing on the landing pad, using its rocket motor as a brake.

New Shepard rocket and capsule, after a test flight

↑ The New Shepard launcher lands under its own power (see yellow arrows, 5). The tourist capsule returns separately, landing under a set of large parachutes (6).

WHAT'S NEXT FOR BLUE ORIGIN?

Beyond New Shepard are two much bigger rockets, the New Glenn and New Armstrong. All are named after 20th century American astronauts.

Similar to rival company SpaceX, Blue Origin builds its own rocket motors, and designs its spacecraft to be reusable.

SPACEPORT EARTH

Several countries could have their own spaceports by the 2030s. Tourist flights to space could be big business by then.

→ Would I need a passport to space?

There are no countries in space, so you would not need a passport for a brief Earth-to-space hop. However, space tourist companies will want to provide lots of souvenirs for your trip, so posters, bags, badges, T-shirts, and other items will be an important part of the flight package. In the future, passports may be needed when flights to space hotels, or the Moon and Mars, are established.

↑ The spaceport at **Houston, Texas, has room for space launches, test equipment, and research efforts.**

← **Virgin spacecraft can be serviced in this large hangar, a building that houses aircraft.**

→ How long will a space flight last?

There may be delays because of technical issues, so take-off may not be a quick process. But spacelines are aiming for a smooth and trouble-free experience!

→ Will all spaceports look the same?

No, just as no airports or harbors are identical. However, spaceport basics will be similar. All will need to have engineering facilities for spacecraft, and reception areas for passengers.

↑ Spaceport America is in New Mexico. It has several floors, and spacecraft are serviced at the bottom.

In 2006, Anousheh Ansari became the first female space tourist on the ISS

WHAT DO YOU THINK?

Many people cannot afford a vacation here on Earth, let alone being able to buy a space flight.

Are space flights luxuries that are valuable only to the wealthy? Or, are they valuable for the work they provide in a high-tech industry?

Flights to the Karman line are just the start for space tourism. In the future, there will be trips to orbit and beyond.

Moon flights could be popular in the late 2020s

➜ What spacecraft will we use?

The SpaceX company has the Falcon Heavy launch rocket. It is powerful enough to send the seven-seat SpaceX Crew Dragon spaceship to the ISS, or past the Moon.

↑← The SpaceX Falcon 9 rocket (above) forms the basis for the Falcon Heavy (left), which can launch a Crew Dragon to space.

➜ What is the Crew Dragon?

It is a follow-up from the cargo-only Dragon capsule that SpaceX developed for supply missions to the ISS. **NASA** has helped, by providing finance and approval for these cargo flights.

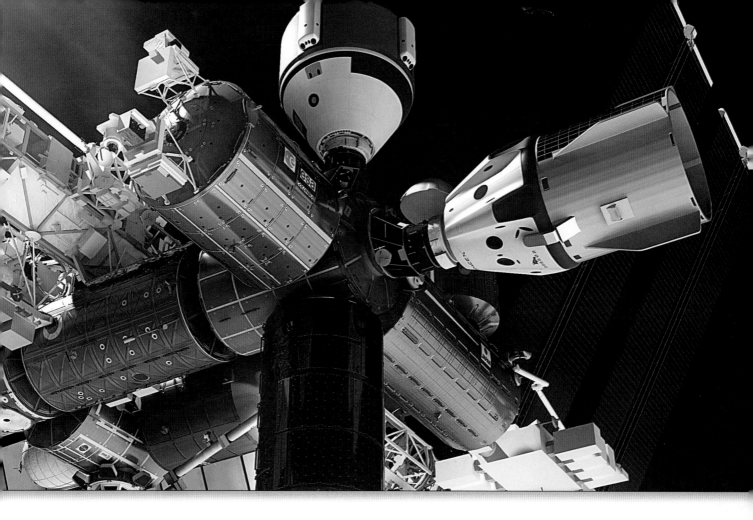

→ What makes the Crew Dragon so special?

For a start, it can carry up to seven people. The **Apollo** Moon missions of 1969-72 used a capsule that could take just three astronauts. Crew Dragon also has four pairs of SuperDraco rocket motors around the sides. These can quickly boost the craft and its crew to safety, in case of a failure with the Falcon Heavy rocket during launch—usually the most dangerous part of a space flight.

↑ Flights to the ISS usually take about three days, from launch to docking.

→ How big is the Crew Dragon?

The spacecraft measures 27 feet (8.1 m) long, which includes a rear section, called the trunk. This has fold-out solar panels to supply electricity, and radiators to keep the spacecraft cool in flight.

WHAT'S NEXT?

In the future, SpaceX may use bigger craft to make landings on other worlds. Rockets could be used to make powered landings, rather than using large parachutes.

HOTEL IN SPACE

Giant space hotels are a dream for the future. Bigelow Aerospace has made a start with its inflatable space structures.

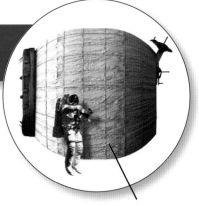

Bigelow inflatable module

→ When will a space hotel be built?

US hotelier Robert Bigelow has been funding experimental space habitats for a number of years, starting with the Genesis 1 of 2006. This was built as a pre-packed "soft" module, which could expand like a balloon once in orbit.

↑ **The Bigelow BEAM, seen here docked to the ISS.**

→ Is there a Bigelow habitat at the ISS?

Yes. The Bigelow Expandable Activity Module (BEAM) has been docked to the ISS since 2016. Instead of the metal skin of other ISS modules, BEAM is made mostly of multiple layers of fabric and foam. These materials are said to be safer and stronger.

→ What happens after BEAM?

Bigelow has plans for much bigger expanding space structures, which could mark the start of a space hotel industry.

Each B330 module (right) has a weight on Earth of about 22 tons (20 tonnes). When expanded in space, a B330 will provide about 11,654 **cubic** feet (330 cubic m) of living space, about the same as a suburban bungalow, or single-story home.

The plan is to dock two or more B330s together, making enough room for a crew to live aboard, and also for space tourists.

→ A three-module B330 group, with a SpaceX Crew Dragon spacecraft docked at one end.

→ Where will the B330 be launched?

Bigelow has plans for B330 modules that will orbit Earth and later, the Moon.

If these are successful, then the B330 could be used for a space hotel orbiting the planet Mars. Other versions could be used on the surface of the Moon or Mars, so providing many comforts of home.

YESTERYEAR'S VISION OF THE FUTURE

Space tourism is not a new idea, though inflatable habitats were not featured in early science fiction stories.

However, a hotel on Mars (right) was drawn by artist Frank Hampson in 1952.

Some details of his art were accurate, such as the gravity pull that tourists would feel. On Mars you would weigh just 38 percent of your weight on Earth.

MENU AT THE SPACE HOTEL

A vacation in a space hotel will mean eating and drinking in a completely strange environment.

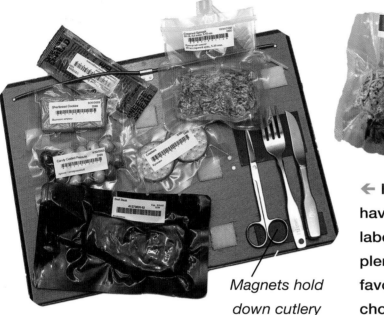

Huge, rotating space hotels will remain pure sci-fi for decades to come

← ISS foods have clear labels, with plenty of favorites to choose from.

Magnets hold down cutlery

→ What will we eat at a space hotel?
Menus will likely follow the experience of crews on the International Space Station. Food is mostly pre-packed (left) and frozen or dried, for storage. But there's plenty of choice, with usually 100 or more items ready to prepare.

Canadian astronaut Chris Hadfield juggles with weightless fresh tomatoes

→ What about choosing fresh foods?
Fruits such as oranges are carried on ISS supply flights, and are prized by crews. Fresh foods will be on the menu of a space hotel that orbits Earth, because supply flights will take only about three days.

→ Will bread be on the menu?
Crumbs are a danger if you breathe them in, or if they float into, and clog, delicate equipment. So only flatbreads such as tortillas have been eaten in space so far.

However, the German company Bake in Space is working on a recipe and a bread machine that will allow ISS crews to make tasty, crumb-free fresh bread loaves.

← A greenhouse module could be a good place to grow fresh food supplies for people on Mars.

In this image, a range of herbs and green vegetables grow in racks. Artificial light boosts the weak Martian sunshine.

→ Could I eat in a hotel on the Moon or Mars?

An essential aim on distant worlds will be to grow fresh produce, and a supply of water will be vital for this.

The Moon has quantities of water, frozen in some icy-cold shadowed craters. And we know that the planet Mars has plenty of water, frozen in the large ice caps of its polar regions.

TOURIST PLAYTIME?

A space hotel will be an ideal place to enjoy living in free fall. Like a full-time astronaut, you'll be able to do simple science experiments, such as checking out your upside-down **refracted** image in a floating bubble of water (right). For safety, the hotel will have a special waterproof section, to avoid accidental damage to electronic machinery.

RESCUE IN SPACE

Danger in space is always an issue. A disaster can result from an explosion, a leak, or even a small problem with a vital component.

→ Have astronauts ever been killed?

Spaceflight is risky, and will probably remain so. The two worst accidents are the 1986 and 2003 US Space Shuttle disasters, when all seven people on each flight were killed. However, space tourist companies will do all they can to keep flights and passengers as safe as possible.

← A Soyuz spacecraft is always docked at the ISS, in case the station needs to be evacuated.

→ Will space tourists be able to use a lifeboat?

The International Space Station already uses the Russian Soyuz spacecraft for this. At least one Soyuz stays docked for about six months at a time, ready to return an ISS crew to Earth at short notice. Future tourists should have seats on the spacecraft ready for them.

→ How many people does a Soyuz carry?

A Soyuz has seats for three, so some crew members—the ISS holds up to six—might have to stay, until another spacecraft can be launched.

← In the future, the ISS may have more than one type of space lifeboat. Here a Soyuz (far left) is accompanied by an automated Dream Chaser spaceplane. Plans for this seven-seater include ISS missions in the mid-2020s.

→ Are there other rescue methods?

While in Earth orbit, another spacecraft could be launched to help at fairly short notice, perhaps as little as a few days.

But once a spacecraft goes further into space, to the Moon or beyond, then the chances of rescue are very low.

So all spacecraft systems have to be designed for safety, both for astronauts and tourists. Any emergency has to be dealt with on board, rather than waiting for any assistance from Earth.

ESCAPE FROM SPACE?

How would you like to abandon ship by wearing this futuristic reentry suit?

The front of the suit would be a rigid, heatproof ceramic shell, similar to the **heat shield** of a full-size spacecraft. The suit's back would be made of multiple layers of super-strong **kevlar** material, covered with flexible metallic foil. After the long fall to Earth, a parachute would open, for a soft landing.

SPACE CRUISE

Browsing a future vacation brochure could mean making plans to visit distant worlds in the **Solar System.**

➜ Where could we go for a space vacation?

If present plans succeed, then exciting but brief up-and-down flights below orbit won't be enough for many space tourists. Others may grow tired of spending long periods in an orbiting space hotel.

Instead, adventurers will want to leave the Earth-Moon system behind, and travel into deep space. And that means destinations such as the planet Mars, or perhaps the mysterious moons of Jupiter, the biggest planet in the Solar System.

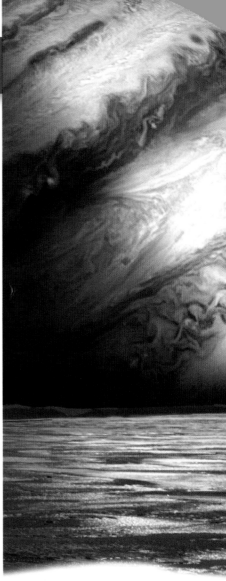

⬆ A space-tour ship sets down on Europa, one of the icy moons of Jupiter. Tourists may explore the vast oceans that lie deep below its surface.

EXPERIENCE THE MIGHTY AURORAS OF JUPITER

EUROPA
DISCOVER LIFE UNDER THE ICE

⬆ Future Solar System tour posters, as imagined by scientists at NASA.

➜ What is the best cruise ship for deep space?

A space cruise ship does not exist yet, but a possible craft could look like the huge Interplanetary Transport System (ITS) ship, envisioned by Elon Musk and his SpaceX rocket company. If built, an ITS could take up to 100 people per flight, perhaps to **colonize** the planet Mars. This won't be for many years, but a space cruise version could follow.

➜ Why would I want a vacation to see other worlds?

Space tourists are likely to go for much the same reason as today: curiosity. Here on Earth, cruise ships allow us to see far-off places such as Antarctica, or Alaska. The tourists of tomorrow may get the chance to enjoy a safari in space, finding out about new worlds in their space cruiser.

➜ Will space tours ever become a reality?

People including Jeff Bezos, Richard Branson, and Elon Musk are working hard on the idea. If they succeed, touring other worlds could become more than a dream of science-fiction writers.

FIVE STAR FUTURE?

Bigelow modules may be used in the future across the Solar System. One could orbit Mars (right) to be used as a short-stay hotel by tourists, before they visit the surface below.

SPACE ELEVATOR

In the future, a trip to a space hotel may be a simple elevator ride away. That's the plan behind technology that could eventually replace rocket launchers.

Ultra-strong carbon materials may make an elevator possible in the future

→ What is a space elevator?

The idea to build an elevator all the way between Earth and space seems simple. To go up or down it, passengers could ride in electric elevator cars. We cannot yet build such a structure, but there are ways to build a shorter version.

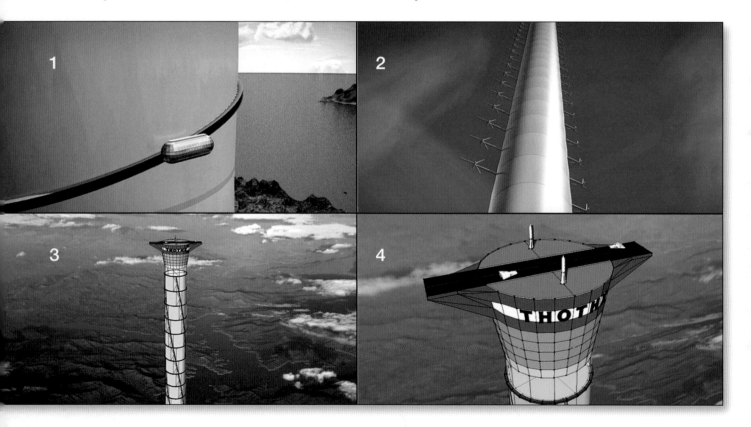

→ What does Canada's Thoth Technology offer?

Canadian company Thoth aims to build towers just 1-10 miles (1.5-15 km) high. At the top will be a spaceport, plus other facilities such as a hotel. The tower is meant to take the place of a launch rocket's first stage. Thoth claims that this could lower today's launch costs by about 30 percent.

↑ An elevator car (1) travels up a Thoth tower. Power comes from **wind turbines (2)**. At the top **(3)** are launch pads and a runway, used by rockets and spaceplanes **(4)**.

⬇ In this future scene, an Elevator Delivery Corporation (EDC) car arrives at the Hotel Orbital, far above Earth (bottom right).

In the car are 30 passengers. Some are workers, ready for transfer to deep-space missions. Others are space tourists, ready to start a week's vacation away from Earth.

COULD WE BUILD AN ELEVATOR TO ORBIT?

Far higher than even a Thoth tower lies the true space elevator, a slender link between our planet and orbital space, about 22,000 miles (36,000 km) away.

It's not possible to construct an elevator today, but the Japanese Obayashi Corporation believes that it will be able to do so by the year 2050. Experimental materials are already 100 times stronger than steel cable, and Obayashi foresees many more developments to come.

GLOSSARY

Ansari XPRIZE A prize offered by XPRIZE, a non-profit foundation for technological advancement. It was backed by Iranian-American Anousheh Ansari.

Apollo The NASA space program that took humans to the Moon. Six landings were made, from 1969-72.

capsule A type of spacecraft without wings. It re-enters the atmosphere blunt-end first, being protected by a heat shield.

carrier plane An aircraft that lifts a spacecraft to altitude, where it is released, to fly with its own engine

colonize To populate or have control over an area

cubic A unit of measurement equal to a cube with sides one foot, meter, or other unit long

dock Airtight latching system that allows two spacecraft to link up, or attach together, in space

gravity ('G') The force of attraction between objects. The gravity on Earth's surface is 1G.

heat shield Protection on the outside of spacecraft protection from the heat of entering the atmosphere. A heat shield is usually made of ceramic material.

↑ **A Virgin Mother Ship carries the VSS *Unity* until it is released.**

International Space Station (ISS) A base that orbits Earth and holds a crew of up to six astronauts

kevlar A super-strong plastic fiber, used where light weight and strength are needed

Karman line Boundary between the air and space, 62 miles (100 km) up

NASA National Aeronautics and Space Administration, the US space agency formed in 1958

orbit A curving path through space by one object around a bigger one, such as the ISS around Earth

refraction The bending of light as it passes through a transparent substance, such as water or glass

rocket A motor that burns a mixture of fuel and oxygen, which are carried in separate storage tanks

solar panel Material that converts the energy in sunlight to electricity

Solar System The Sun and planets, plus moons, comets, asteroids, and other space matter

Soyuz Russian spacecraft that brings cargo and people to the ISS

weightlessness Also called "free fall," when objects can float freely

wind turbine Propeller-like system that captures the energy in moving air, and converts it to electricity

People mentioned in the book:

Ansari, Anousheh (1966-) Iranian-American, co-backer of the Ansari XPrize. Stayed as a "space participant" on the ISS in 2006.

Baturin, Yury (1949-) Russian cosmonaut. He has flown to space twice, including as Flight Engineer with Dennis Tito, in 2001.

Bezos, Jeff (1964-) American founder of Blue Origin

Bigelow, Robert (1945-) American hotelier and pioneer of inflatable living modules in space

Binnie, Brian (1953-) American test pilot who flew SpaceShipOne to take the Ansari XPrize

Branson, Richard (1950-) British founder of the Virgin Galactic space tourism company

Hadfield, Chris (1959-) The first Canadian to walk in space. He has also been a commander of the ISS.

Hampson, Frank (1918-85) British creator of the sci-fi hero Dan Dare, for the best-selling Eagle comic

Karman, Theodore von (1881-1963) Hungarian-American physicist, for whom the Karman line is named

Lindbergh, Charles (1902-74) An American aviator, who flew non-stop from New York to Paris, in 1927

Melvill, Mike(1940-) South African-American test pilot, who flew the SS1 to the Karman line, in 2004

Musabayev, Talgat (1951-) A cosmonaut from Kazakhstan, who has flown to space three times

Musk, Elon (1971-) South African-born, Canadian-American founder of the SpaceX rocket company, and other high-tech ventures

Peake, Tim (1972-) British astronaut on the ISS from 2015-16

Rutan, Burt (1943-) American aerospace engineer. He has created many unusual aircraft, as well as SpaceShipOne and Two.

Tito, Dennis (1940-) American engineer who became the first space tourist, on the ISS, in 2001

Winne, Frank de (1961-) Belgian astronaut, presently with the European Space Agency

Acknowledgements
We wish to thank all those people who have helped to create this publication.
Individuals:
  Frank Hampson/Eagle
  David Jefferis
  Gavin Page
  Pat Rawlings/NASA
  Keith Tarrier/Fotolia
Organizations:
  Bake in Space GmBH
  Bigelow Aerospace
  Blue Origin
  Boeing Corp
  Canadian Space Agency
  ESA European Space Agency
  Houston Spaceport
  JPL Jet Propulsion Laboratory
  Lockheed Martin Space Systems
  NASA Space Agency
  NASDA, JAXA, Japanese Space Agencies
  Obayashi Corp
  Roscosmos Russian Space Agency
  Sierra Nevada Corp
  SpaceX
  The Spaceship Company
  Thoth Technology
  Virgin Galactic
  XPrize Foundation

ABOUT THE AUTHOR

David Jefferis has written more than 100 non-fiction books on science, technology, and futures.

His works include a seminal series called World of the Future, as well as more than 30 other science books for Crabtree Publishing.

David's merits include the London Times Educational Supplement Award, and also Best Science Books of the Year. Follow David online at: www.davidjefferis.com